DROMAEOSAURUS

and Other Dinosaurs of the North

by Dougal Dixon

illustrated by
Steve Weston and **James Field**

PICTURE WINDOW BOOKS
Minneapolis, Minnesota

Picture Window Books
5115 Excelsior Boulevard
Suite 232
Minneapolis, MN 55416
877-845-8392
www.picturewindowbooks.com

Printed in the United States of America.

Library of Congress Cataloging-in-Publication Data
Dixon, Dougal.
Dromaeosaurus and other dinosaurs of the North /
by Dougal Dixon ; illustrated by Steve Weston &
James Field.
p. cm. — (Dinosaur find)
Includes bibliographical references and index.
ISBN-13: 978-1-4048-2745-5 (hardcover)
ISBN-10: 1-4048-2745-5 (hardcover)
1. Dromaeosaurus—Juvenile literature. 2. Dinosaurs—
United States—Juvenile literature. 3. Dinosaurs—
Alberta—Juvenile literature. I. Weston, Steve, ill. II.
Field, James, 1959– ill. III. Title. IV. Series.
QE862.S3D5935 2007
567.9097—dc22   2006012133

Acknowledgments
This book was produced for Picture Window Books by
Bender Richardson White, U.K.

Illustrations by James Field (pages 4–5, 7, 11,
15, 19) and Steve Weston (cover and pages 9,
13, 17, 21). Diagrams by Stefan Chabluk.

Photographs: Eyewire Inc. pages 8, 18, 20;
iStockphoto pages 6 (Jason Cheever), 12 (Stefan
Steinbach), 14 (Tom Lewis), 16 (Michael and
Michelle West); Frank Lane Photo Agency page 10
(Michio Hoshino).

Consultant: John Stidworthy, Scientific Fellow of
the Zoological Society, London, and former
Lecturer in the Education Department, Natural
History Museum, London.

Reading Adviser: Susan Kesselring, M.A., Literacy
Educator, Rosemount–Apple Valley–Eagan
(Minnesota) School District

Types of dinosaurs
In this book, a red shape at the top of a left-hand page shows the animal was a meat-eater. A green shape shows it was a plant-eater.

Just how big—or small—were they?
Dinosaurs were many different sizes. We have compared their sizes to one of the following:

Chicken
2 feet (60 centimeters) tall
6 pounds (2.7 kilograms)

Adult person
6 feet (1.8 meters) tall
170 pounds (76.5 kg)

Elephant
10 feet (3 m) tall
12,000 pounds
(5,400 kg)

TABLE OF CONTENTS

WHAT'S INSIDE?

Dinosaurs! These dinosaurs lived in what is now northern North America. Find out how they survived millions of years ago and what they have in common with today's animals.

LIFE IN THE NORTH

Dinosaurs lived between 230 million and 65 million years ago. The world did not look the same then. Today, Alaska and Canada are covered with huge areas of snow and ice. At the end of the Age of Dinosaurs, northern North America had open plains, with enough plants for all sorts of dinosaurs to eat.

Herds of all kinds of dinosaurs moved across the northern plains, including horned *Pachyrhinosaurus* and *Anchiceratops*, and duck-billed *Edmontosaurus*. The dinosaurs were looking for new feeding grounds.

5

PACHYRHINOSAURUS

Pronunciation:
PACK-i-RYE-no-SAW-rus

Pachyrhinosaurus was a horned dinosaur. Its horns were on an armored shield around its neck. It also had a bony lump on its nose. *Pachyrhinosaurus* lived in large herds. Its fearsome look kept predators away.

Herds today

Bison live in large groups and are always on the move to find new food supplies, just like *Pachyrhinosaurus* was.

Size Comparison

Sometimes, *Pachyrhinosaurus* swam across rivers. Many of the dinosaurs did not survive the difficult journey.

EDMONTONIA

Pronunciation:
ED-mawn-TOE-nee-uh

Some dinosaurs had armor all over. *Edmontonia* was one of these. Its neck, back, and tail were covered with armor plates. It also had spikes sticking out of its shoulders. *Edmontonia* ignored other dinosaurs, as no other animal could harm it.

Protection today

Porcupines are well protected against enemies, like *Edmontonia* was. Instead of armor and spikes, a porcupine is covered in sharp quills.

Size Comparison

Edmontonia was safe from any other dinosaur in the far North—except other *Edmontonia*! Males may have used their spikes in fights. The males fought over females or to be the leader of the herd.

ANCHICERATOPS

Anchiceratops had three horns on its head. It had a pair of long horns above the eyes and a short horn on the nose. It also had a narrow shield around the neck. This made *Anchiceratops* look bigger and fiercer than it really was.

Horns today

The musk ox has long horns, like *Anchiceratops* did. It uses them in battles and to defend itself against an attacker.

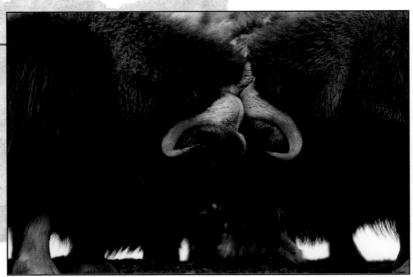

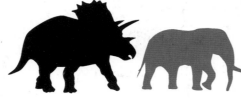

Size Comparison

When *Anchiceratops* fought, they locked horns with one another and pushed. The loser backed away without being hurt.

DROMAEOSAURUS

Pronunciation:
DROH-mee-o-SAW-rus

Dromaeosaurus was the fastest dinosaur of the far North. It chased after smaller animals with its long legs. *Dromaeosaurus* killed its prey with the sharp claws on the second toes of its feet. It used its long jaws and sharp teeth to eat.

Clawed hunter today

The lynx hunts animals that are smaller than itself. It kills them with its long claws, like *Dromaeosaurus* did.

Size Comparison

Dromaeosaurus had great eyesight, like an eagle or owl. It used its sight to hunt for little animals running among the plants.

13

EDMONTOSAURUS

Edmontosaurus was a duck-billed dinosaur. It had a ducklike beak, or bill, for a mouth and jaws. It fed on the few conifers that grew on the plains. It used its bill to strip bark from the trunks and to pull cones and needles from the twigs.

Bark-eaters today

The beaver feeds on parts of trees. It uses its strong front teeth to strip away bark and gnaw at wood, like *Edmontosaurus* did.

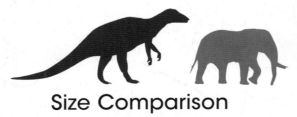

Size Comparison

Edmontosaurus wandered between the conifers of the plains, looking for tree parts that were good to eat.

15

Kritosaurus was another duck-billed dinosaur. It had a crest on its head that it used for signaling to other dinosaurs. Each kind of duck-billed dinosaur had a different shaped crest. This allowed the animals to recognize one another.

Head ornaments today

The pronghorn is a plant-eater of the plains, like *Kritosaurus* was. It has a pair of horns on its head instead of a crest.

Size Comparison

Kritosaurus was able to reach down and eat the low-growing plants that covered the plains of northern North America.

17

THESCELOSAURUS

Pronunciation:
THES-ki-lo-SAW-rus

Thescelosaurus was a medium-sized dinosaur that could run fast. At times, it may have moved on all four legs, rather than on its hind legs alone. Its skin color blended into the surrounding plants, allowing the dinosaur to hide from enemies.

Fast runner today

The white-tailed deer is a shy animal that runs and hides from enemies, like *Thescelosaurus* did. Its long legs give it great speed.

Size Comparison

Thescelosaurus hid from the big meat-eating dinosaurs of the time. If it saw a predator, *Thescelosaurus* would run away.

Some dinosaurs had a bony lump on their head. The biggest of these bone-headed dinosaurs was *Pachycephalosaurus*. It used the bony lump to ram into other dinosaurs. *Pachycephalosaurus* also had a group of spikes and horns on its head.

Battering rams today

The bighorn sheep has a pair of enormous horns on its head. Like *Pachycephalosaurus* long ago, it uses its head structures to crash into enemies.

Size Comparison

When one *Pachycephalosaurus* was angry with another, it would crash headfirst into the side of the other dinosaur to drive it away.

21

WHERE DID THEY GO?

Dinosaurs are extinct, which means that none of them are alive today. Scientists study rocks and fossils to find clues about what happened to dinosaurs.

People have different explanations about what happened. Some people think a huge asteroid hit Earth and caused all sorts of climate changes, which caused the dinosaurs to die. Others think volcanic eruptions caused the climate to change and that killed the dinosaurs. No one knows for sure what happened to all of the dinosaurs.

GLOSSARY

armor—protective covering of plates, horns, spikes, or clubs used for fighting

bill—the hard front part of the mouth of birds and some dinosaurs; also called a beak

conifers—trees that produce seeds in cones and have needle-like leaves

crest—a structure on top of the head, usually used to signal to other animals

herds—large groups of animals that move, feed, and sleep together

horns—pointed structures on the head, made of bone

plains—large areas of flat land with few large plants

prey—animals that are hunted by other animals for food; the hunters are known as predators

signal—to make a sign, warning, or hint to other animals

To Learn More

At the Library

Birch, Robin. *Hard-Headed Dinosaurs*.
Philadelphia: Chelsea Clubhouse Books,
2003.

Clark, Neil, and William Lindsay. *1001 Facts
About Dinosaurs*. New York: Backpack
Books, Dorling Kindersley, 2002.

Cohen, Daniel. *Pachycephalosaurus*.
Mankato, Minn.: Bridgestone Books, 2004.

On the Web

FactHound offers a safe, fun way to find Internet
sites related to this book. All of the sites on
FactHound have been researched by our staff.

1. Visit *www.facthound.com*

2. Type in this special code
   for age-appropriate
   sites: 1404827455

3. Click on the FETCH IT button.

Your trusty FactHound will fetch the best sites
for you!

Index

Look for all of the books in the Dinosaur Find series: